Praise for Voices at Twil

"*Fascinating. Howe's carefully documented accounts of these old towns' histories and present states of being are beautifully deepened by the photographs and her excellent, moving poems, haunting in their own right, bringing lost places and people back to vivid life on the page, in the mind. I didn't want it to end, and can only hope Lori Howe will do this again, and again.*"
—**Brad Watson, author of *Aliens in the Prime of Their Lives* and *Miss Jane: A Novel***

"*Lori Howe blends guide-book practicality with evocative poetry, photographs, and personal reflection to summon faded Wyoming towns existing on a blend of history and hope. From her offerings we glean that places can be both ghost and solid flesh, often simultaneously.* "
—**Julianne Couch, author of *The Small Town Midwest: Resilience and Hope in the Twenty-first Century***

Lori Howe's Voices at Twilight is an enchanting companion for those seeking a deeper understanding of the reasons and ways of the American frontier. From the beehive kilns of the "true ghost" Piedmont, to living museums like Centennial, " the wind's mad bride, shredding her garments into prayer flags", the prose will sweep you away on a site to site road trip under the big sky, across the vast abandon of the prairie. Having reached each long forgotten outpost, Howe's arresting poetry will hold you up at the edge of town, apprehended as a character in the story, standing half-lonely and half in love with "the Opal wind that shoves a hand in every pocket".
—**James Scott Smith, author of *Water, Rocks, and Trees***

Lori Howe has captured Wyoming's history of great gain and great loss in words, images, and emotion. There are few pieces of literature that can bring back to life the past and this is a remarkable mix of history and poetry. I am so pleased she has written this book and I hope all Wyomingites relish its beauty and emotional qualities. I hope this book will encourage people to get off the beaten path and experience places from the past. Many of them are part of the Wyoming State Park, Historic Sites, and Trails program, are listed on the National Register of Historic Places, and are accessible to the public.
—Mary Hopkins, historian

Voices at Twilight

Voices at Twilight

A Poet's Guide to Wyoming Ghost Towns

Lori Howe

Sastrugi Press

San Diego • Jackson Hole

Sastrugi Press / Published by arrangement with the author

Voices at Twilight: A Poet's Guide to Wyoming Ghost Towns

The author has made every effort to accurately describe the locations contained in this work. Travel to some locations in this book may be hazardous. The publisher has no control over and does not assume any responsibility for author or third-party websites or their content describing these locations, how to travel there, nor how to do it safely.

Any person exploring to these locations is personally responsible for checking local conditions prior to departure. You are responsible for your own actions and decisions. The information contained in this work is based solely on the author's research at the time of publication and may not be accurate. Neither the publisher nor the author assumes any liability for anyone exploring the locations described in this work.

Sastrugi Press
2907 Iris Avenue, San Diego, CA 92173, United States
www.sastrugipress.com

Library of Congress Catalog-in-Publication Data
Library of Congress Control Number: 2016936093
Howe, Lori
Voices at Twilight / Lori Howe - 1st United States edition
p. cm.
1. Poetry 2. History 3. Poetry—Women Authors
Summary: Voices at Twilight invites the reader into the in-between world of past and present in this collection of poems, historical essays, and photographs, all as hauntingly beautiful and austere as the Wyoming landscape they portray.
ISBN-13: 978-1-944986-01-8
ISBN-10: 1-944986-01-4

811.08'

Printed in the United States of America

All GPS coordinates in World Geodetic System 84 (WGS 84)

Available in print, ebook, and audio book formats

10 9 8 7 6 5 4 3 2 1
Front and back cover: Piedmont, WY; Photographs by Erik Molvar
Photographs are the author's unless otherwise noted
Cover design: Nancy Takeda

For Erik, Kimberly, Leif, and Jasmine

and in loving memory of Anna Stong Bourgeois, who so
loved the high plains

Table of Contents

WYOMING

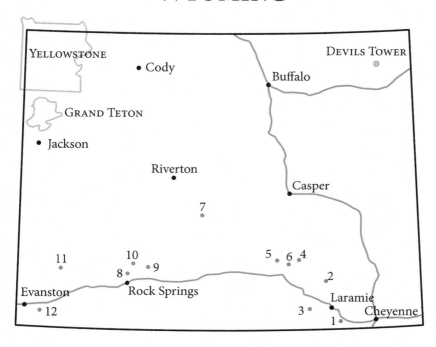

Towns on map

1.   Old Sherman
2.   Bosler
3.   Centennial
4.   Medicine Bow
5.   Hanna
6.   Old Carbon
7.   Jeffrey City
8.   Reliance
9.   Superior
10.   Winton
11.   Opal
12.   Piedmont

All history is multi-faceted, and there are as many unique versions of it as there were people alive to tell the tale. The historical essays contained herein represent a good-faith effort to present generally agreed-upon true histories of these towns and their people. The author asks that readers consider the accumulation of twice-told tales, myths, legends, and campfire stories surrounding the history of Wyoming and its settlement when reading this book.

Introduction

When I wrote *Voices at Twilight*, I hoped this book would help to extend the existence of some of Wyoming's most unique and at-risk ghost towns and town sites that will likely cease to exist in the next decade. For towns that still exist but are locked into the dead-end cycle of bust, I wished to give them back the glory of their boom days, if only on the page, and give readers entrance into the history and essence of all of these places.

I also hoped that the book would serve as a literal guide for readers who seek out these towns for themselves, and offer the experience vicariously for those who prefer to explore these towns through their own imaginations and mine. *Voices at Twilight* fills a void in the literature about Wyoming's ghost towns, offering a human and intimate perspective that differs from the guidebooks and historical documents that fill the shelves of local bookstores throughout the region. The historical essays provide the life stories of these towns; the poems, their essence.

Whether you explore these ghost towns through the words and images in this book, or use *Voices at Twilight* to help you find them on your own, I hope it also helps you feel their accumulation of lives, of fortunes made and lost, and of all the hopes and ambitions settlers have carried with them to the high plains of Wyoming.

There are, of course, many more ghost towns in Wyoming than those I included in this book. I chose the ones I wrote about based largely upon their abilities to amaze me; Old Carbon, for example, was built many miles from any source of civilization, in full knowledge that there was no water. The towns along the Lincoln Highway, such as Bosler, Medicine Bow, and Hanna, are living memories of the first east-to-west highway to cross America from coast to coast. Old Sherman, Wyoming, was a train stop on that rail line, and was for a time one of the highest train towns in the world, at over 8,000 feet.

Jeffrey City bears skeletal testimony to the dangers of depending upon a single, capricious industry to support a full and thriving town; when the uranium market disappeared after the Cold War, the population of Jeffrey City simply evacuated the town and left it sitting vacant in the desert. Superior, Wyoming, is a town built into the sides of a box canyon so narrow that the roads are all one-house deep. Winton, Wyoming almost defies description. It seems impossible that a town once existed at the Winton site; it is so remote and inhospitable that it is difficult to imagine people once lived there. However, there are old photographs of Winton that show blooming flower gardens and lush lawns and trees, neat, orderly houses, businesses, and schools.

Nearby Reliance relied so entirely upon its coal tipple that the entire population of the town lobbied to have their tipple registered as a National Historic Place after it became disused. The ghost town of Piedmont is another monument to indomitability and industry; the charcoal kilns and the Byrne family so engraved that brief valley with the legacy of their names and history, it feels as though time hangs suspended in the sheltered lee of the mountain. Opal, Wyoming, is a place as desolate and ugly as its name is lovely.

The order of appearance of the towns in *Voices at Twilight* is from east to west, along Interstate 80 and the Old Lincoln Highway, route 287 and Highway 30, and occasional detours north or south, to Hanna and Jeffrey City.

Whether you use *Voices at Twilight* as a guidebook to help you find the ghost towns and see them with your own eyes, or choose to see them through my words and photos, I hope *Voices at Twilight* gives you, as it has me, the chance to feel more deeply the essence of Wyoming and her landscape—often harsh, always beautiful—and the courageous people who have passed through here and put down roots.

OLD SHERMAN

41°08.138'N 105°24.046'W

Old Sherman is located in the southeast corner of Wyoming, 17 miles east of Laramie. Exit I-80 at Vedawoo Road, exit # 329, turn right and drive south on the Ames Monument Road for 2 miles. Just before the Ames Monument parking lot, turn right onto an unmarked dirt road and follow it northwest for ¼ mile. Look for the tiny cemetery inside a chicken-wire fence. Most of Old Sherman's few foundation stones are due northwest, on the other side of the road.

Sherman was founded by the Union Pacific as a railroad stop in the late 1860s, and by 1874, had developed into a substantial town at 8,262 feet. As a result, it held the romantic distinction of being the highest train stop town on the entire continent. Reality was less romantic. The location and elevation ensured constant, often gale-force winds, drifting snow, and scouring summer heat, as well as few amenities. Nevertheless, Sherman appeared in travel stories and newspapers published across the country.

Sherman's lifespan was cut short in 1901 when the Dale Creek Embankment, a route with a shallower grade, was constructed and the rail line relocated. There were no mineral deposits at Sherman, so when the railroad departed, Sherman was soon abandoned for lack of an economic base.

Ironically, what is left to mark Old Sherman's location is a monument to two brothers, Oliver Ames, Jr. and Oakes Ames, who was a congressman from Massachusetts. The brothers had amassed a substantial fortune after taking over their father's coal shovel business. They became interested in the Union Pacific railroad after discovering the government was funneling substantial subsidies toward its construction. The Ames brothers managed to acquire control of the Union Pacific railroad, and bought a financial company that they renamed Credit Mobilier.

Shortly thereafter, the two Ames-held companies were doing business with each other. Credit Mobilier held the contract for 667 miles of rail to be laid. They also hid a profit of over fifty million dollars in government subsidies allocated for that construction. The *New York Sun* broke the story, implicating James Garfield, the Vice President of the United States, Speaker of the House, and future President of the United States. Several other highly placed government officials were named, too. The charges against these highly respected men were all the same: having taken bribes from the Ames brothers for the allocation of railroad subsidies.

The allegations were never substantiated, and the case never went to court. In the wake of these deals, however, the Ames brothers' reputations were ruined. The politicians in question emerged largely unscathed. Around this time, the Union Pacific fell heavily into debt. Crucial government subsidies, once promised to the Ames brothers, were quietly reallocated elsewhere.

By this time, the Ames Monument, a stone pyramid adorned with bas-reliefs of Oliver and Oakes, had already been constructed. It is an ironic pile of rock, immortalizing only the Ames brothers' greed and dishonesty, as the railroad is no longer within sight of the monument. Even Old Sherman is gone with scarcely a trace.

The Ames Monument, moot though it's been for well over a century, remains stolidly on the barren prairie. Over the decades, the stone faces of the two Ames brothers have lost most of their features, due to both erosion and vandalism. Even a century later, Oliver and Oakes are remembered as the brothers who nearly derailed the U.P. It is a mystery why the monument was left standing. It would have been relatively easy to dismantle it. A truer monument lies nearby.

The town site of Sherman has nearly disappeared, except for the small cemetery. This small plot contains several headstones but officially, only one set of remains—those of the infant boy, Lester Hegkert. Born in Sherman in 1882, the tiny boy died there less than a year later and was interred in the town's cemetery by his father, Daniel M. Hegkert. There is no official record of why the tiny boy's remains were left behind when others were claimed and relocated. Logically, it holds that two of the many, unmarked graves in the Sherman cemetery may have held Lester's parents.

Historians believe the cemetery once held the remains of 12 females and 41 males. Still others insist that some of the unmarked graves were not exhumed. Are tiny Lester's parents still there with him? Or, as most historians claim, was he indeed left in this cold, scoured landscape all alone?

The real story about poor little Lester's parents may never be known. Was his mother a seamstress or laundress at the hotel, or perhaps a soiled dove or saloon girl? Did she die during childbirth, or did she leave her child with his father and seek her fortune further up the rails? Did his father, Daniel Hegkert, die on the rails, or did he move on after burying his son, never to return? Or, as some have speculated, could Lester's parents only afford one enduring headstone, and choose it for their infant son, rather than for themselves? It is entirely possible that the whole family lies undisturbed in the Sherman cemetery, sharing one stone, carved remarkably deep to endure.

Full, preserved records of the lives and deaths of travelers and workers across the high plains are relatively few. No matter what happened to Lester Hegkert's parents, neighbors and visitors regularly leave small toy trucks, colorful pinwheels, and teddy bears on Lester's grave. These small tokens left behind for a child are a far greater monument to the impact of railroad construction in places as harsh and unlivable as Old Sherman. They mark this place as uniquely human.

Other remnants of Sherman include the foundation for the water wheel and a scattering of other, possible foundation stones, largely obscured by sagebrush. In old photographs, the Sherman waterwheel shines in the sun beside the tracks like a Ferris wheel, lending a lightness and hope to the landscape. Deep, round holes in the stones show the wear they endured to hold the waterwheel in place in such wind.

Standing amidst the few objects that indicate the site was once inhabited, I think of Sherman's lively role in those newspaper stories. It offered good rooms and meals to travelers. The town supplied amenities to the Union Pacific employees who lived there. I think of the famous Susan B. Anthony, traveling across the continent by train in 1872, staring out the thick, glass windows at the impervious mountain pass, wondering what lay ahead. She spent several January days trapped in a snowstorm just outside of Sherman, including one harrowing day with the train stopped inside a snow tunnel. Her diary of the trip contains the following descriptions:

January 2: *Still stationary. The railroad company has supplied the passengers with dried fish and crackers. Mrs. Sargent and I have made tea and carried it throughout the train to the nursing mothers. It is the best we can do...This is indeed a fearful ordeal, fastened here in a snowbank, midway of the continent at the top of the Rocky mountains. They are melting snow for the boilers and for drinking water.*
The train has moved up to Dale Creek bridge and drawn into a long snow-shed. Here we remained all night and, with the rarified air and the smoke from the engine, were almost suffocated, while the wind blew so furiously we could not venture to open the doors.

January 4: *Morning found us still at Sherman and we did not move till 1pm...Halfway to Granite Canyon the snowplow got off the track and one wheel broke, so a dead standstill for hours.*

January 5: *Bright and beautiful. Reached Cheyenne at 11:30am.*

The area around Old Sherman is stark and quite lovely in a rocky, austere way, but not all who have visited have found it so. In 1892, Robert Louis Stevenson wrote about Sherman and environs in his book, *Across the Plains* (Chattus & Windus, London, 1892):

To cross such a plain is to grow homesick for mountains. I longed for the Black Hills of Wyoming, which I knew we were soon to enter, like an ice-bound whaler for the spring... The plains have a grandeur of their own; but here there is nothing but a contorted smallness. Except for the air, which was light and stimulating, there was not one good circumstance in that God-forsaken land.

Of all the ghost towns along the southern corridor, Sherman is one of the most deteriorated. Even Old Carbon, situated on a desolate stretch of prairie with neither shelter nor shade, still bears the stone walls that once protected its inhabitants. There is not a stick of Sherman left to be found without a determined search. There are scarcely any shards of dishes, pieces of glass bottles, or metal findings here. The few cracked foundation stones, spotted with orange lichen, seem more a product of glacial shift than human fortitude.

The town site, scoured clean by time and wind, has neighbors now. The conveniences of the Interstate, four-wheel-drive vehicles, and a twenty-minute commute to Laramie have combined to give this area a rebirth in the last decade. Long driveways lead off the Ames Monument road, and those who long for space and quiet, a removal from town, have found their own peace here. For Sale signs, though, flank many of these driveways. Several buildings are mere shells, abandoned before they could be finished. Note: the town site of Old Sherman is now on private property. If you visit, please respect this and stay on the trails.

The view from Old Sherman has not changed, though.

Across the furrow of the Interstate, the scrub sage mountains of the Laramie Range absorb the weather. Austere, beautiful, inscrutable, it is a landscape that lures but does not welcome.

Note: Please see book's webpage at www.sastrugipress.com for additional links and information.

Old Sherman

In photographs curling
with age,
Sherman's windmill shines,
floating
over the granite bones of the plain,
a Ferris wheel
catching the afternoon sun.
Beneath its wooden legs,
two hotels, a saloon,
a mercantile and post office
watch gusts blow off
nameless peaks to the North.
Etched in sepia,
men in suits and hats
stand still in the short street;
a dark-haired woman
in a long dress
floods the walk
with what might have been blue.

In 1865, Sherman
was the highest train town
on the coast-to-coast railroad,
noted by travel writers
for its hotels,
good beds with a desolate view.
When the railroad shifted

three miles South,
Sherman stood for decades,
empty,
before it realized it was dead
and lay down
inside its reliquary
on the high plains.

Today,
the town's reduced to
six massive stones
that held the windmill erect.
If you look carefully
you can find shards and bones of Sherman
woven into the tough, wheaten grass—
bits of colored prairie glass,
cans and mechanical arms
so oxidized, they flake in the wind.

In a cemetery the size of a bed,
one headstone marks the grave
of an infant son,
left behind when the others were taken.
Today, as sunlight thickens
with blowing snow,
the baby's stone peers through
the soft gray screen,
out across the harsh beauty
of rock and twisted pine,
watching the shiny beetles

of far-off cars
trace the interstate,
their drivers ignorant of this tiny ossuary,
the lonesome grave of a child
tended by strangers
in this dry crease of rock and sand.

Ames Monument Road, Old Sherman townsite

View of Old Sherman Townsite

Photo: Erik Molvar

Sole Remaining Grave, Old Sherman Cemetery, Old Sherman

BOSLER

41°34.567'N 105°41.717'W

Bosler is located on both sides of the Lincoln Highway, Route 30/287, 28 miles west of Laramie, Wyoming, and 20 miles east of Rock River, Wyoming.

The town is named for early Wyoming ranching baron, Frank Bosler. Owner of an extensive business empire including ranching and mining concerns, Bosler was sometimes described as Wyoming's Rockefeller, or a J.P. Morgan. Although Frank Bosler was generally considered an honorable business-man, his partnership with John C. Coble was a venture that brought him to the edges of infamy.

Coble, the one-time owner of the iconic, legendary buck-ing bronco, Steamboat, was a close, personal friend of the infamous Tom Horn. In fact, the Bosler/Coble business part-nership fell asunder when Coble allegedly misused $100,000 of company funds to pay for Tom Horn's defense when he stood accused of murdering 14-year-old Willie Nickell on July 18, 1901.

Horn was an infamous cattle "detective" employed by cattle

barons during Wyoming's tumultuous range wars. During this time, the cattlemen employed hired guns such as Horn to track down cattle rustlers and exact frontier justice. Ella Watson, otherwise known as Cattle Kate, was the victim of such a lynching by cattlemen, although there is no evidence that Tom Horn was involved. After the lynching of Cattle Kate and her partner, James Averell, the cattlemen's association seized their property. This action served to plant seeds that would explode into the Johnson County War.

It is worth noting that, by all accounts, Ella Watson was innocent of any involvement in cattle rustling. The mania of the cattlemen to preserve their faltering empire drove them to terrible deeds. Tom Horn, though he described himself as a "detective," was an instrument of that empire, and as unsavory a character as any who appear in the lore of early Wyoming. The names of John C. Coble and Frank Bosler will forever be associated with his infamy; indeed, after Horn was hanged, Coble's fortunes deteriorated. He shot himself in the lobby of a hotel in Elko, Nevada in 1914.

Steamboat, the bucking bronco, was reportedly born on the Two Bar Ranch near Bosler, Wyoming. The horse went on to great fame despite the association with Coble. Steamboat was eventually owned by Cheyenne Frontier Days, and was reportedly buried on the Frontier Park grounds—an honor not awarded to any other animal, before or since. Beyond his death, the iconic image of this charismatic, bucking bronco lives on as an enduring symbol of the West. Adopted by the University of Wyoming, it is still pictured on Wyoming license plates.

Bosler, Wyoming, led a colorful, vibrant life long after Frank Bosler, Coble, and their associates passed into history.

The town enjoyed boom years as a stop on the heavily traveled Lincoln Highway during the 1930s, 40s, and 50s.

Today, most of this town is uninhabited. The man who claims to own Bosler, an unusual person referred to locally as 'Doc,' does live there. Rumors about his lifestyle are like antelope in Wyoming: always running amuck in town. If his life has been as interesting as rumors paint it, he has been a Hell's Angel, a minister, a drug kingpin, a limo driver, a millionaire, a mayor and an adult film star. In the controversial film, *The Laramie Project*, Doc is played by Steve Buscemi. For such a small, apparently abandoned town, Bosler can lay claim to an abundance of historical and contemporary fame and infamy.

Reports vary on the current ownership of Bosler. According to the Albany County Assessor's Office, Bosler was once a platted city. Now, it is an abandoned, vacant piece of land. Its individual plots of land are considered 'salvage lots' that are valued at less than one hundred dollars each. This legal definition of Bosler's status was published in the year 2000. Nowhere in the legal document is a single owner mentioned.

The town site itself is not on private property, according to the County Assessor's office, though there are some privately owned residences on either side of the highway. In spite of this, some resident's protective impulse toward the town has led him or her to shoot skunks. The reeking corpses are sprinkled inside the abandoned structures to repel tourists. One of the most intact structures, the old library, was burned to the ground in 2010.

There was never mining activity at Bosler. When the Union Pacific stop was eliminated, the town began its decline. The grocery store, diner, café, Laundromat, and gas stations closed. Finally, the motor inn failed. Residents loosed their hold on the village and left.

It is unfortunate that the atmosphere in Bosler is so unwelcoming. It is a gem, with many houses and other structures left basically just as they were when abandoned, down to dishes in the sink and clothes in the closets. The old library was particularly well preserved and I feel its loss keenly.

Unfortunately, in 2013, arsonists burned some additional surviving structures, but many survived. Bosler, with so many intact artifacts, is a fascinating experience for the ghost town enthusiast and for historians of the high plains.

Bosler was founded along the path of the Lincoln Highway and the Union Pacific railroad. It enjoyed its boom years as a shipping hub and a tie siding, a place where railroad ties were massed and stored. However, the Interstate's path to the south shifted most of the traffic away from the town.

In its prime, Bosler was a complete community, with orderly streets stretching out across the prairie on both sides of the Lincoln Highway. There were over a thousand residents in Bosler at this time, up until the 1930s. As it died away, most residents shifted 28 miles east to Laramie.

There are buildings from several periods of construction readily visible from the highway, such as a 1930s era motor motel and several dilapidated houses. A solid, two-story brick school house was built by hand by the townspeople of Bosler during the boom years. Other remains include an interesting shack that housed men and women's restrooms and is covered with faded advertisements.

There are also many examples of antique cars and trucks in the meadow adjacent to the site of the former library. These hulking shapes, though they are rusted and their windows fractured, have the ghosts of road trips on the first coast-to-coast highway in their cracked rear-view mirrors. Beneath the warped and faded surface of this town, you can still see and feel the youthful hope of prosperity and progress that the Lincoln Highway brought here.

After the tie siding was moved and I-80 stole away most of the automobile traffic in 1972, Bosler held on as a town of ever-decreasing population. Classes were held in the school until the early 1980s, when enrollment petered out and all the children went to Laramie for school. One business, Doc's Furniture Store, remained open on a limited basis into the 1990s, but has been closed for over a decade.

If you choose to go ghost town hunting in Bosler, please be careful where you explore. Even if the abandoned buildings are accessible, rotting floors and staircases present real risks. Also, there are a handful of occupied residences on both sides of the highway and railroad track.

Like other ghost towns, Bosler is a repository of secrets and stories left untold. Unlike most other ghost towns, Bosler's secrets and stories aren't lost in the past. In this ghost town, wind may not be what moves a curtain. It's a place where your imagination may whisper to you that someone is watching your every step. Chances are, someone is.

Bosler

Where the cold arm of the Snowy mountain
thins to wrist and river,
Bosler's people changed into antelope,
locusts and rain ate the paint from her walls.
Now vacant stores sell beds for ghosts,
and the school instructs winter
in the habits of crows.

Foundations flake away
like yellowed pearls of glue
in photo albums, memories of a youth
in which everything is still to come,
the roads ahead wide open
and going everywhere,
bathed in a Technicolor shine
almost certain
to endure.

In Spanish, the word *naufragio*
means shipwreck,
and *sobreviviente*, survivor.
Here on the edge of the sage,
tv antennae and broken lightbulbs
broadcast stories of some hardy few
who clung on longer to Bosler than most.
They wait for the golden eyes
and lonesome, smoke-filled voices of trains,

their cars, stacked like children's blocks
in red, green, and blue,
the only riot of sound and color
left here on the border
dividing nothings.

Now, the wide, empty pavement
and glassless windows
stare back, mute chronicles
of a long-forgotten Rapture,
not a single willing tongue left to sing
of a prosperous heaven
or its soft and verdant grace.

Photo: Erik Molvar

Surviving Structures, Bosler

Photo: Erik Molvar

Abandoned Automobiles, Bosler

Photo: Erik Molvar

Surviving Structures, Bosler

CENTENNIAL

41°17.833'N 106°08.310'W

Centennial is located just west of Laramie at the foot of the Snowy Range on scenic byway Highway 130. To visit Centennial, follow Snowy Range Road from Laramie to the Highway 130/230 split and take the right spur. Follow Highway 130 27 miles west to Centennial, which is situated on both sides of the highway. Be aware that the speed limit drops sharply as you enter town. Centennial is fully alive, with business and residential districts, as well as a lively arts and culture scene.

Before the Transcontinental Railroad came through Laramie in 1868, Centennial Valley was a seasonal home to nomadic Plains Indian tribes. Cheyenne, Arapaho, Crow, Shoshone, and Sioux lived in the area. White settlers were newcomers to the area. They struck out from Laramie to harvest the abundant timber growing on what is now known as Centennial Ridge.

With the advent of the railroad, its workers, tie cutters, and their families settled in the Centennial Valley. Tie camps were the first established settlements at the foot of the mountains. The 1862 Homestead Act drew ranchers to the relatively lush Laramie River Valley. When gold was discovered on Centennial Mountain in 1875, the tie camps evolved into a permanent town site, situated at an elevation of 8,076 feet. In 1876, the town was named to commemorate the nation's first centennial celebration.

As was all too common, reports of the gold vein's depth and quality were greatly exaggerated. Though the initial investment in the Centennial mine was nearly a million dollars, the vein ended at a fault line. Many prospectors searched for its continuance on the other side. The rest of the gold vein, if indeed it exists, has never been found.

A silver boom held brief sway in the 1890s, but actual silver production was limited. Logging and ranching continued in this area of great natural abundance. These industries are mainstays of the local economy to this day. However, a Pine beetle infestation threatens the future of logging in this area of the mountain west.

Despite its isolated location at the base of the Snowy Mountain Range and long, cold, snowy winters, Centennial has been home to colorful folks such as the Self family for many generations. Pat Self owned the first Buick dealership in Laramie. His son, Murry "Murf" Self, described Pat as the Great Gatsby of Wyoming. Pat Self, who owned the Old Corral restaurant, was known for falling asleep and wrecking his beloved luxury automobiles. He is remembered for many things in Wyoming, including surviving rollovers and crashes into bridge abutments that would certainly have killed a less lucky driver.

The entire Self family has left a lasting, vibrant legacy in

Centennial. Murf's mother, Nici Self, is widely known as the mother of the train depot museum. After the Union Pacific decommissioned the Centennial train station in the 1960s, she persuaded the U.P. to deed the building to the town of Centennial as a museum. In the following years, this became a trend across the west. The railroad deeded numerous decommissioned train stations to towns as museums. The Nici Self Museum is a gem. Any visit to Centennial is enriched by a stroll through the unique buildings on the site.

Nici Self was a pen pal of novelist James Michener. When the Self family donated a historic log cabin as a public library for Centennial, Michener traveled to Centennial for the library's dedication. Locals wanting autographs besieged him. During his visit, he toured the old silver and gold mines with the Selfs. Their old propane-fueled vehicle broke down, and they and Michener had to hitchhike back to town for the library's dedication—just in time for the train to come through town and drown out Michener's speech.

In a letter long ago lost to fire, Michener wrote to Pat Self of the great impression Centennial's hospitality and mountaineer spirit made on his life. The feeling was apparently mutual. A great many Centennial residents proudly display their signed copies of Michener's books. Murry "Murf" Self continues the colorful family legacy as a long-time resident, business owner, and ambassador of Centennial life.

Many of these stories of Centennial and the Self family are available as Wyoming Stories audio recordings on the Wyoming Public Radio website. See the book's webpage for the audio link.

Today, Centennial is a living ghost town whose population fluctuates around 200. Centennial's citizenry are hardy, interesting souls occupying a collection of historic, period, and modern buildings. They are presumably great aficionados of snow and winter weather, both possible any day of the year. To date, the snowiest year on record for Centennial was 1951. Locals look forward to the winter that will break that old record of 200 inches in a single year.

In winter, the town hosts several snow- and winter-related events, such as cross-country skiing Poker Runs and a Christmas Fair. Permits are available at the Forest Service office for those who enjoy the family tradition of snowshoeing into the forest above Centennial to cut down their own Christmas tree.

The beautiful green valley tucked in at the base of mountains strewn with pristine lakes. In summer, it offers recreation areas for camping, hiking, biking, kayaking and fishing. In winter, cross-country and downhill skiing, snowshoeing and snowmobiling abound.

Art galleries, good food, live music, a Sunday farmer's market, and dinner theatre add to the attractions of this little mountain hamlet. Adventure seekers and families return time and again. Old gold mine sites are still scattered in the mountains above the Centennial Valley, and some prospectors are still certain that there's yet gold to be found. Beyond logging and ranching, Centennial now relies upon tourism.

Established in 1907, the Historic Mountain View Hotel offers lodging. A bed and breakfast housed in the original post office, established in 1867, is another place to stay. More modern accommodations are available at the Old Corral and the Friendly Store.

Dining options include the Historic Trading Post, the Mountain View café, the Friendly Store café, the Bear Tree Tavern, and the Old Corral. In the summer, farmers and flea markets are held on weekends at the Bear Tree Tavern. Live bands, indoors and out, liven the market throughout the year.

In 2000, the Wyoming Geological Survey reported the presence of gold in a sample of rock taken from Centennial ridge. Perhaps the ghost vein long sought by prospectors is just waiting to be discovered.

Centennial

Centennial is the wind's mad bride,
shredding her garments
into prayer flags
on this first day of Spring.
Her fine bits of glass and silver
polished blind by sand and time,
she waits for veins of gold
to work closer to the surface,
like a sliver in her small brown foot.

She's dropped scraps of red and blue
—an old milktruck, a gas pump,
geraniums in coffee cans—
trailing bright behind her
in a bottomless self-portrait,
washed cool and lovely by her weather.

In the melt of afternoon,
she shakes snow from her hair
—bright shower down the mountain—
and hums a song for the end
of another Winter.

Downtown, Centennial

Downtown, Centennial

Photo: Erik Molvar

Centennial

Photo: Erik Molvar

Creeping fox, Centennial

MEDICINE BOW

41°53.922'N 106°12.060'W

To visit Medicine Bow, follow the Lincoln Highway (state route 287, Highway 30) 57 miles west from Laramie, Wyoming.

Medicine Bow, Wyoming, like many others along the Lincoln Highway, is a town waiting for another boom. It began as a tie siding, a gathering point for railroad ties that were floated down the Medicine Bow River. In the 1860s, the Union Pacific Railroad laid track alongside the Medicine Bow River. In 1868, the U.P. set up a water tank and rail station to supply its locomotives. A town gradually formed, and Medicine Bow became a cattle shipping hub, as well.

Over time, the timber business dwindled and failed, as did the mining booms in surrounding mountains. The town experienced a boom as a stop along the busy Lincoln highway. Unfortunately, it suffered another blow when I-80 opened in the early 1970s, 35 miles away, and diverted much of the Old Lincoln Highway's traffic. In the late 1970s, uranium and coal mining in the area around Medicine Bow gave its economic status a short-lived boost.

Since the 1980s, Medicine Bow's population has dwindled to around 200, though wind energy has recently discovered the place. The area south of Medicine Bow is statistically one of the windiest places in America. The U.S. Bureau of Reclamation funded the first experimental wind turbine project in 1982. Since then, additional wind fields have been constructed relatively near the town, making Medicine Bow a convenient place for wind farm employees to live.

Still, there is no visible sense that another boom is in motion for Medicine Bow. Unprotected from wind and weather on the open plains, it has a worn-out aspect, and most of its businesses are long-closed and apparently abandoned. The town's distance from other, larger settlements make it a treacherous and expensive commute. The hotel, museum, gas station, and liquor store appear to be the only services and sources of employment, other than the wind industry.

The Medicine Bow buildings along Highway 30 represent many periods in the town's history. The most famous, and visible, edifice in Medicine Bow is the Virginian Hotel, an impressive, three-story stone building erected when most structures were small and made of wood. It is named for the protagonist in Owen Wister's western novel, *The Virginian*, though there is no evidence that the author ever set foot in Medicine Bow.

The Virginian hotel is an interesting stop for anyone passing through, as it generally has vacant rooms for history buffs and tourists to view. It is decorated in a 1900s bordello style; less synthetic velvety wallpaper and fewer dusty, fake flowers would be an improvement. The restaurant on the ground floor is consistently open in the summer; call to be sure in the off season. There is an informal diner as well as a more formal, Victorian dining room for dinner.

The town's only open bar is located on the east side of the hotel's ground floor; it is a good place to have a beer and listen to stories. The bar itself is said to be crafted of the longest single piece of jade in the world. The bartender will tell you about the time Christopher Reeve was stranded there in a snowstorm. You'll also be welcome to tour the upper floors of the hotel and perhaps catch a glimpse of Hal, the hotel ghost.

At one time, the Virginian Hotel was truly a fine establishment in Medicine Bow. It was a sign of affluence and prosperity. It seemed to cement the town's success and permanence in such an isolated area along the new Lincoln Highway.

Now, ghost hunters best know it as the home to Hal and other lingering spirits. Unexplainable cold spots manifest throughout the hotel, and apparitions have appeared in several rooms and on the staircase. Hotel staff report hearing faint music from another era in the parlor, as well as finding objects in odd places, perhaps moved there by restless spirits. Paranormal investigators report high levels of ghostly activity throughout the hotel at night.

Solidly built as it is, ghosts or no ghosts, it will likely overlook the Lincoln Highway for another hundred years. The Virginian's renown will continue to draw western history and ghostly phenomena buffs to Medicine Bow.

The Medicine Bow Museum, located in the old train depot right across from the Virginian Hotel, is another well-preserved and maintained structure. It is a repository of information about Medicine Bow, surrounding towns, and early life on the high plains. The original Owen Wister Cabin was relocated to the grounds of the museum by the Wister family, and is a worthwhile stop for fans of the western novel.

Medicine Bow has perhaps 200 year-round inhabitants. Although the choices may be slim, you will find gas, food, and lodging here, as well as many excellent stories from long-time residents. Seven miles east of Medicine Bow, you'll find the Como Bluffs Dinosaur Museum/Fossil Cabin. Though rarely open, it is still a fascinating place to stop for a walk or picnic.

Medicine Bow fits the description of a 'semi-ghost.' It remains inhabited and has a few services, but has lost its primary employment, revenue sources and the majority of its population.

Nevertheless, past and present residents of Medicine Bow remain loyal to the place. An atmosphere of pride and nostalgia permeates the town. There is a communal sense of identity amongst those who live or once lived there. It is difficult, mentally and physically, to live in a tiny town on the prairie, so far from other settlements.

In winter, drifts and scouring wind meet little resistance. The area surrounding Medicine Bow looks like the surface of the moon—featureless, bare expanses of glaring white for mile upon mile. It is not unusual for Highway 30 to be closed for days at a time in the vicinity of Medicine Bow, either by snow or by spring flooding. For that time, Medicine Bow is shut off from the outside world. There is an air of proud self-sufficiency about this town and its inhabitants. This, more than anything, suggests that Medicine Bow may defeat the odds and survive.

Medicine Bow

Thaw.
The highway disappears
beneath a pale silk slip of run-off,
unknown depths enticing.
Tulips stutter up the sides of the ditch,
bright punctuation in yellows
and reds.
The prairie is soaked and half-frozen,
the air, hot and green with waking sage.
Steam rises from wheel-cuts
lingering on roads.
The sun trembles down the Virginian Hotel
in wet, light streaks of melting ice,
stretching out on steps
bleached bone-dry by dusk.

Medicine Bow is a song
caught between stations,
its melody out of tune.
Pale and bedraggled,
left behind by winter,
all its light bulbs hang cracked
and vacant,
its hidden streets stretching
from the main road, unplowed,
like uncut leaves
in a water-stained book.

Photo: Erik Molvar

Entering Medicine Bow

Photo: Erik Molvar

Springtime, Medicine Bow

Downtown, Medicine Bow

Photo: Erik Molvar

HANNA

41°52.250'N 106°33.751'W

To visit Hanna, 70 miles west of Laramie, Wyoming, exit I-80 at the Hanna/Highway 72 exit, or follow Highway 30/287 west, from Laramie, which is scenic and adds 7.3 miles to the trip.

The town of Hanna, Wyoming, was founded in 1889, in part as a shrewd political move by the Union Pacific Railroad's Mark Hanna. Infighting amongst white and Chinese miners had recently resulted in the infamous Chinese Massacre in Rock Springs. It fell to Mark Hanna to address similar rumblings and threats of violence amongst the miners at Carbon. With the advent of this new mine site, he sought to staff the Hanna coal mines with Black and Finnish workers. He hoped they would not mix with the English speaking miners, join the union, or strike.

Despite Mark Hanna's efforts, violence and death were realities in the town that bears his name. In 1889, a train collided with a caboose filled with miners, killing Joseph Diamond instantly and severely injuring several others. The injured men were transported to Laramie and attended by Dr. Finfrock, a name still familiar in southeast Wyoming.

The train incident fanned the flames of discontent between the workers and the railroad. The conductor, Woodmansee, as well as the engineer, fireman, and brakeman, all fled for the mountains as a rope was secured and the threat of lynching became real. After he turned himself into the sheriff in Rawlins, the grand jury refused to indict the engineer, Dan Haskins. None of the other trainmen were charged.

Explosions also plagued the Hanna mines. In separate disasters in 1903 and 1908, explosions that caused extensive cave-ins killed nearly 300 miners.

The Hanna 1 Mine, site of these two disastrous explosions, was closed in 1908. A treasure trove of meticulously preserved documents, accounts, and photographs of Hanna during the mining boom years are available, courtesy of Wyoming historians. See this book's webpage for the latest links with more information.

Over the last century, mining ventures have struggled on, but Hanna is another boom town in the attenuated process of going bust. Like Bosler, Medicine Bow, and Rock River, Hanna keenly felt the abrupt loss of Lincoln Highway traffic when I-80's trajectory wooed away travelers.

As the Lincoln Highway was, until I-80 opened, the most used route across Wyoming's southern corridor, the loss of traffic meant a loss of business and revenue. Hanna's livelihood, though, was always largely dependent upon mining.

So, in spite of the loss of Lincoln Highway traffic, Hanna boomed on into the 1950s, producing coal and employing miners from all over the world. Hanna's cemetery is a study in ethnic diversity. Chinese, Japanese, Swiss, Greek, Ukrainian,

Polish, Czech, Italian, Swedish and African miners came to the high desert of Wyoming to live and work. Some of them left surprising legacies.

The son of a Greek immigrant, internationally famous, abstract sculptor Peter Forakis was born in Hanna, Wyoming in 1927. He spent the first ten years of his life there while his father worked the mines. The Forakis family then moved to California. Although the sculptor made his career in New York and California, his time on the Wyoming prairie and on the seas with the Merchant Marines made lasting impressions on his art. In his austere, geometric designs made with found timber, as well as industrial metals, the imprint of the high plains and the coal mines persists.

This ghostly imprint lingers for all who visit. Hanna sits just under 7,000 feet, on a treeless, barren, gusting plain. It is a feckless, hard-edged place with little beauty or grace to recommend it. Even when new, the first houses in Hanna were small, cheaply built, and poorly insulated. In the intervening years, trailer homes replaced construction, though they are poor shelter from arctic winters and arid, shadeless summers. Over half the houses, trailers, and barbed plots of vacant land in Hanna are staked with For Sale signs, many of them sunbleached and illegible with age.

Hanna's coal mine boom lasted until 1954, when the Union Pacific switched to oil power, and the town was virtually abandoned. A brief resuscitation occurred in 1979, when Arch Mineral opened a surface mining operation. Though it employed nearly 600 men, the town failed to regain the ground it had lost. The population never recovered. Today, minimal surface mining continues. The town claims a population of over 800, though that appears to reflect pride and nostalgia more than an actual census.

The most interesting things in Hanna are the layers of period architecture that rise up the terraced hillsides, demarcating boom and bust cycles in the town's history. A wind-scoured hilltop cemetery sits just west of town. There is a small but beautifully maintained and well-staffed museum by the railroad tracks at 502 Front Street.

Remains of the once vital Japanese village are lamentably scattered and few. Archeologists studying Hanna in the distant future will, no doubt, attempt to explain the windowless tarpaper shack, insulated with newspapers and straw, sporting two satellite dishes and a 1980s baby-blue Jacuzzi outside. They will exhibit photographs from 1908 that show the neat, verdant rows of the Japanese town garden. The contrast between them and the garish palm trees spray-painted on the cracked façade of the bar is striking.

While the vast majority of Hanna's citizenry are outward bound, some few are returning. Having spent decades away, some folks are moving back to Hanna to retire, and they predict yet another rebirth for this hardscrabble town. It has, after all, earned the moniker "the town that wouldn't die," and created boom after boom, dragging itself forward by way of opportunism and sheer force of will.

Perhaps, in this age of sustainable resource development, Hanna will harvest assets that never run dry. Few other places are so wealthy in relentless wind and sun.

Hanna

Hanna was never lovely
or shaped like a violin,
not even when her dresses
were new, when her shoes fit,
when pockets were full
and men in suits hovered,
wanting.

Hanna has been in the sun
too long,
waiting,
counting on nothing,
leaning against the walls of the mine.

Hanna is still waiting
for someone to buy her a drink
as she sits at the bar,
squinting through cigarette smoke,
wearing stale perfume
and dangling For Sale signs
like plastic earrings,
waiting for an offer
come twenty years too late.

Photo: Erik Molvar

Long View, Hanna

Photo: Erik Molvar

Mine Disaster Monument, Hanna

Photo: Erik Molvar

View of Elk Mountain at Twilight, Hanna

Photo: Erik Molvar

St. Park's Episcopal Church, est. 1922, Hanna

OLD CARBON

41°50.880'N 106°22.560'W

To visit Old Carbon, take US-287/N US-30W 66.1 miles from Laramie to County Road 115. Old Carbon is located 5.1 miles south on CR 115, through private land. This location is particularly isolated and the terrain difficult. The road is unimproved and largely impassible from November to April or May.

Old Carbon, Wyoming, is a true ghost. Unlike many of the other ghost towns along the Old Lincoln Highway, there are no surviving structures or residents in this defunct coal town at 6,831 feet. It was home to as many as 3,000 people during its boom years. Isolated, harsh, and barren, it is nevertheless my favorite of Wyoming's ghost towns. I find myself visiting it again and again, even in winter, when I have to make my way to the town site by cross country skis.

Carbon was founded as a coal mining town in 1868, to supply the Union Pacific Coal Company. In fact, for much of Carbon's existence, there was no road to the town. The railroad spur that led into Carbon was the only way in and out.

Carbon's location was utterly inhospitable to humans. There was no water source at Carbon. Barrels of the precious stuff were hauled in at considerable effort and cost from Medicine Bow.

The town site is on the open plain, with no trees whatsoever for building materials, fuel, or shade. In winter, there is nothing to stop the wind, and ten-foot drifts are common. In summer, the lack of water and shade combine with gritty, scouring wind. In Carbon's boom years, its residents faced all these challenges along with frequent Indian attacks. The entire population often had to sleep in the mines, under guard. By several different accounts, the first person laid to rest in the Carbon cemetery was the victim of an Indian attack.

Even with the modern conveniences of four-wheel drive vehicles and satellite phones, Old Carbon is still daunting and inhospitable. It is nearly impossible to comprehend the challenges faced by those who built the town, board by board, stone by stone.

The landscape resisted the town every step of the way. The wind dismantelled the first structures even as they were being built. These boards, of course, were purchased at significant cost, as there were no trees for miles. Many people lived in sod-covered dugouts, and were often surprised by a human or bovine foot penetrating their roofs.

In spite of the climate, Indian attacks, and other challenges, Carbon thrived. Miners of Chinese, Canadian, Czech, Swedish, Hungarian, Italian, Greek, Japanese, and Welsh descent made their way to this tiny town in Wyoming. Cultures intertwined. In addition to the seven coal mines, Carbon supported a lively town. The general store, eight saloons, two churches, a school, a hotel, rooming houses, a newspaper, an opera house, and a miner's hall were all built by hand.

The town burned nearly to the ground twice. An over-turned lantern started the second fire in one of the rooming houses and spread across the entire town. Lack of water caused residents to fight the fire with gunpowder. After that, the town was rebuilt out of stone.

Carbon thrived until 1899, when coal production in the mines began to decline. By 1902, the coal deposits were de-pleted, and the last of the seven mines closed. The railroad moved the Carbon spur to an easier grade. As great deposits of high-grade ore were discovered at Hanna, Carbon was rendered a place of the past.

Remaining wooden structures at Carbon were moved to Hanna, including the Miner's Hall, when the majority of the miners relocated to the new mines. The Miner's Hall, the larg-est movable structure in Carbon, was physically carried across the prairie to its new location in Hanna by the many miners who built it. They ran logs beneath the structure, lifted and carried it the twelve miles over land to Hanna. Unfortunately, as the museum staff at Hanna informed me, the Miner's Hall burned to the ground in the 1980s.

The best-preserved remnant of Old Carbon today is its aus-tere, beautiful cemetery filled with exquisitely carved stones, many in ornate family plots. Infants occupy a terrible per-centage of the graves in the Old Carbon cemetery, and a great many of the others buried there are women who died in child-birth. They are joined by a great many miners who perished in accidents, fires, and explosions. Beyond the cemetery, the layout of the town is still visible in a large array of crumbling sandstone walls and foundations. The streets, now reduced to dirt paths, are marked here and there by historical signposts.

Carbon did have a doctor for part of its lifespan. For the most part, serious illness or accident in Carbon carried a high risk of fatality. It was simply too isolated a settlement with too limited access to the outside, for help to arrive in the event of emergency. The cemetery is an eloquent, mesmerizing representation of daily life in Old Carbon.

Old Carbon, in spite of its isolation and harsh conditions, or perhaps because of them, continues to exert an irresistible attraction. There are recent graves in its cemetery, though the town has been gone for over a hundred years. It is an elemental place, with a kind of beautiful, merciless honesty. It is unsurprising that people still choose to be laid to rest there.

Historical markers designate many of Carbon's ruined buildings, but nothing has been rebuilt or restored. Amongst the sandstone and sagebrush, the occasional vintage glass bottle or cast iron handle or door may be seen.

Unfortunately, even though Carbon's isolated location discourages scavengers, many of its artifacts have been pilfered. What remains, for the most part, is glass. To the right of the main road through Carbon is the old business and rooming segment of town. The ground is brightly strewn with weather-smoothed, colored glass of every shade.

Old Carbon

Old Carbon, WY
Part 1: 1869
<u>The Seamstress</u>
Family lost to shipdeath, one by one,
I watched faceless sailors heave
my blood over the rail, into the foam.
The night I turned fourteen
I cut my curtain of hair with a knife,
washed my dead brother in rainwater
and took his clothes.

I worked the railroad as a boy,
helper to the gandies
until my curves gave me away.
Now, this place. Carbon,
a flat stretch of baked earth,
the stink of coal in every stitch,
every bolt of cloth,
every piece of laundry
flinging darkly out
from taut wire.
Nothing here
was meant to last.

This town is a faint scratch
in the desert,
a mercantile with its last seamstress
in the graveyard,

dead of childbirth
and her needles lying idle,
a place so desperate
that water's sound
is a train whistle half a day off—
water's scent is a fresh wooden barrel
pouring out the cool
smell of damp forest
into the hot mouth of hell.

I cannot find sleep
in the darkness.

I shouldn't be down
in the mine
with the women and children
where I can't hear the Indians,
whether they've come or gone.
I've faced down worse men,
to put it plain.

I'm good with a rifle, and true.

The Glassblower

When I was twenty,
a stray gobbet
of fire
took half my vision.
Today, I speak fire's plain language
of heat and breath, of light and quickening.
Bottles and jars are my offspring—

small, clear vessels of blown glass,
ordinary and precious as fingers and toes.

Tonight I stand with the watch,
rake the darkness
with my one good eye
as we wait, feet listening
through our boots,
our charges safe below.
This night, no lanterns are burning
to lure Fate.
With the smallest flame
our town beckons, a lonesome ship
lit for miles on the vast and wine-dark sea
of the plains.

Two years back,
I poured stained glass windows
for the church,
then watched them shatter
in a fire so hot
it inhaled the whole town,
their angels melting back
to steam and cool in the dirt
like blue-green reflections of a heaven
sashed in red
and clouded with violets.

The new church, her deep walls
a foot thick with hardy stone,
awaits the new windows

lying finished in my shed just up the road.
I poured them full as I dared
against the lashings
of wind and winter,
saved precious pigments for a year
as my own offerings to God.

If Carbon lasts the night,
we'll raise them tomorrow.
Darkness shields us little, though,
from those who travel
by horses and starlight.

The Baker
God and I know how many men I've killed,
and their women.
Little ones, too.
Indians all, and war,
but those small faces
are written on the inside
of my skin, salted there
like bones
on the bottom of the sea.

There's no call for a life of prayer
unless you're a priest,
but bread—
God knows there is always a call
for bread,
and mouths to eat it, and amen.

Even now, all the small souls
of Carbon lie safe, asleep, in Mine No. 3.
Steady as an old dog, my rifle at my side,
I wait in the dusky silence of night
for the sound of hoofs in the distance,
war cries nearing us, waking our guns.
The only prayer I breathe tonight
is for the raiding party to pass
east, between us
and Medicine Bow,
that no blood be shed
by my hand
this night.

Tomorrow morning,
some four hours off,
I'll grind winter wheat and pour out
fresh water,
start my ovens fresh,
sweep out the coals,
and bank embers like heaps of gold
until the air fills with that good, right scent
of bread waiting for butter,
waiting for hands to share it,
waiting for mouths.

Even now, the seamstress
sleeps safe, deep in the mine,
the scent of the coal seam
in her red hair.
Close beside her, sharing warmth,

my starter
promises tomorrow and a simple alchemy
of sourdough, the peace of the ovens,
of loaves fresh and fragrant
delivered into good and unstained hands.

Somewhere near,
a coyote whispers to her young,
gathers them close,
feeling the prairie shake
with many horses.

They are coming.

Part 2: 2016
A kinder ocean,
the sage-brush sea
gives back its dead.
Here they sleep in rows,
headstones graven deep,
the last moments of day falling
in gold
across their thinning names,
a lingering of their voices
rising like mist
from the stones
of the church—
a violet evensong
at twilight.

Carbon State Bank, 1881, Old Carbon

Old Carbon Cemetery, Old Carbon

Surviving Church Wall, Old Carbon

Long Way Gone: the road to Old Carbon

Photo: Erik Molvar

JEFFREY CITY

42°29.658'N 107°49.560'W

To visit Jeffrey City, exit I-80 at Rawlins, Wyoming, and take 287 north. Most of the town is located on the south side of Highway 287, near the old route of the Oregon Trail. The nearest city is Lander, Wyoming, sixty miles west on Highway 287.

Jeffrey City, Wyoming began as most mining towns do. A few men saw the gleam of profit just around the corner. In Jeffrey City's case, this gleam was not a reflection of coal values, or even copper or silver, but uranium.

In the mid-1950s, Jeffrey City was born in response to a high demand for uranium, fueled by the Cold War. In a few years, this former Pony Express stop became a full-fledged, modern town. Its sole purpose was servicing and housing the families and workers of the nearby yellowcake uranium mine. Western Nuclear Corporation owned all of it. Elizabeth Pope, writing for McCall's magazine in 1956, called Jeffrey City "The Richest Town in the USA."

Aerial views of Jeffrey City in the 1950s show a green

patch of grass and trees in the midst of desert, asserting a wholehearted defiance of nature. A mix of bachelor's quarters, single-family homes, apartments, businesses, schools, and entertainment complexes fanned out in orderly rows across this platted city. Far from Lander, the nearest municipality, Jeffrey City had to be self-sufficient.

Construction and commerce boomed. In the 1970s, an enormous high school was constructed, along with a recreation center with an Olympic-sized pool. Jeffrey City built hundreds of buildings of all kinds, to hold movie theaters, bowling alleys, hair salons, grocery stores, and even a Weight Watchers. Tree-lined, paved streets edged up to pristine sidewalks and well-tended, verdant lawns bordered with flowers. All construction was modern, most completed in the 1960s and 70s.

Jeffrey City declared itself there to stay. Incongruous as a Hollywood movie set, it seemed to have sprung from the hard dirt overnight. Unbeknownst to most citizens of Jeffrey City, it was to have a total life expectancy of less than thirty years.

At the close of the Cold War, demand for uranium fell to an all-time low. The mines closed. Jeffrey City's sole sustaining industry died. In the early 1980s, the town's population dropped below 100. It steadily decreased in subsequent decades. A small handful of people, a post office, and a Catholic church are the only significant living remnants of this town. The population reached 6,000 only a few decades before.

The bright spot in today's Jeffrey City is Monk King Bird Pottery, owned and operated by Byron Seeley, aka The Mad Potter. It is a good reason to add this town to your trip across Wyoming. Seeley, a thirty-something, latter-day hippie with wild, curly blond hair and a modest, welcoming smile, is a talented potter. He specializes in throwing Red Canyon ware vessels that echo the streaked, sedimentary patterns of canyon walls. Burnt red, ochre, white, and fire black layers of desert clay coalesce to mimic the beautiful, austere landscape. Patterns embedded in their hauntingly beautiful, subtle layers are revealed when the pots harden. At this stage, Seeley uses a sculpting tool and peels the pots. He pulls aside the curtain of the clay's surface to free images of angels, animals, and other worlds hidden deep in the clay. A documentary featuring Seeley's creative process is available on the book's webpage at Sastrugi Press.

Monk King Bird, Seeley's pottery shop, is housed in an old gas station/garage on colorful space filled with Seeley's pottery and paintings. One of the only functioning businesses in Jeffrey City, you'll easily spot Monk King Bird at 23004 Hwy 789. You may want to call before you visit: (307) 544-2213 or check the gallery's Facebook page, Monk King Bird Pottery. The store hours are listed as 6am-9pm daily. According to some reports, what this means is that you are welcome to browse if Seeley is not present. Likely, he'll leave a sign directing you to seek him where he is fishing, hanging out with a next door neighbor, or bellied up to Jeffrey City's lone bar.

If you are fortunate, you may have a chance to watch Seeley throwing a Red Canyon clay pot. You may even be able to make a request and purchase the resulting mug, vase, or urn. These are extraordinary pieces. It is worth a stop in this tiny ruin of a town.

Outside of this truly unique pottery shop, Jeffrey City's particular fascination lies in its wasted youth. It is a ghost town that has not had enough time to fade into the desert. It looks like it should be useful for *something*. Some new boom should come along and shake it out of hibernation, wake up the still viable houses, streets and services again. An artists' colony, perhaps, could build itself up around the Monk King Bird pottery and revive Jeffrey City. The deteriorated state of the existing buildings, along with a near-total lack of services and isolation has discouraged any rebirth.

Sadly, if Jeffrey City cannot find a reason for being, it will continue to slowly, stubbornly, give way to erosion and time. Viewing the remains of the old town is eerie. It is as though the whole area had been contaminated and evacuated. Thoughts of a toxic, abandoned mining towns in rural China come to mind.

The truth is much simpler. In the wake of the collapsing uranium market, the town and mines were sold to U.S. Energy, Inc., which proposed the town first as an ideal site for a state prison, and later as a tourist and recreation spot. Neither idea met with any success.

In the intervening decades, much of the abandoned housing has been dismantled. Some has been torn down. Most of the single-family homes were lifted off their concrete slabs and auctioned for pennies on the dollar to anyone willing to haul them away. Muddy Gap, the nearest town (23 miles east), was a destination for many of Jeffrey City's citizens, houses, and buildings. With the exception of some housing and a few other buildings, Jeffrey City remains largely intact. Street signs, tennis courts, utility poles and cables, and fire hydrants still stand. Worn but serviceable businesses and houses are out there in the desert, waiting to become useful to someone again.

Weather and time have taken a great toll on these buildings. I suspect that most of the housing, now becoming hazardous, will have to be torn down in the next decade. From time to time, a revitalization plan is proposed for Jeffrey City. None have come to fruition. Only action can save this settlement in the vast, scrub-sage desert.

Jeffrey City

The morning gold of the prairie,
soft, before the heat comes,
smooths the wrinkled streets
of the town,
gilds humble phone lines
and street signs,
transfers the dark lines
of swings and slides
into their lightest negative.

A fox rounds a weed-blown fence
with something small and still
in its mouth,
and still the fox is beautiful,
carmine in early light.

In Jeffrey City,
the sky is clean because the wind
meets no resistance,
and the scents of sage and alkali
no longer mingle with coffee,
eggs, cigarette smoke,
the exhaust of cars
warming in driveways.

There are no kettles, no keys,
no lighters or dimes

jangling
in this town:
there are no cars,
no food,
no people.
It is as if all the brick houses
that once edged these sidewalks
were built, unknowing,
along the veins and fingers
of an enormous hand,
and one ordinary morning,
it closed reflexively,
those same pots, keys,
lighters, change, and lives
jangling lightly inside it,
and stowed itself in a dark,
seamless pocket.

Out here,
the desert sings of homecoming
and permanence
with a forked tongue,
spitting rust,
yellowcake,
and peeling paint
down empty streets
paved to last
so much longer
than anyone could live here.

Old service, Jeffrey City

Historic marker, Jeffrey City

RELIANCE

41°40.194'N 109°11.580'W

To visit Reliance from Rock Springs, Wyoming, take I-80 to exit 104, and follow US-191 N 2.9 miles, to reach the Reliance Road. Reliance is located 2 miles north on CO Road 42.

Reliance was named, like everything in it, for the coal company that owned the town. Today it is a semi-ghost with a population of about 300. In the boom days, this town claimed a population of almost 2,000. It weathered several industrial highs and lows before coal lost its power and demand.

It is a small town, now more of a suburb of Rock Springs. Reliance it has a kind of charm and pride of place that asserts its identity as a town in its own right. The streets are narrow, but the houses are well maintained. They are a collection of different architectural styles and eras. Everything is spotlessly clean.

Located in a short, narrow canyon, Reliance claims both shade and character that Rock Springs lacks. It would make a good setting for a novel about ordinary people who find extraordinary grace. The setting would be physically centered on the rusting hulk of the disused coal tipple, like a postmodern metaphor.

Two tipples, the large, box-like metal structures once widely used to sort coal, were constructed during different prosperous periods in Reliance. The Great Depression caused Reliance and its industry to slip into hibernation. The advent of WWII reinvigorated the coal industry and Reliance along with it. A new Reliance tipple was a model of modern innovations, and Reliance enjoyed a second boom during this time.

Unfortunately, the end was near. Like so many towns that supplied water and coal to the Union Pacific, Reliance suffered a deathblow when the U.P. converted to diesel engines. This monumental shift was completed in the 1950s. The mines closed shortly thereafter. The town experienced a sharp decline, though it maintained a population between two and three hundred people.

The Reliance Tipple, though abandoned, was registered as a National Historic Place in May of 1991. It is fenced, with interpretive signs and a walking path around its perimeter. Disappointingly, there are no tours of the facility itself. Coal tipples are rarely preserved beyond their usefulness, and many more historians and tourists would visit Reliance if allowed inside its tipple.

I asked around town, but no one was aware—or perhaps, not forthcoming—of who to ask to arrange a private tour. Perhaps, like many old buildings, it is no longer safe for people to enter. It is a silent monument to the coal boom. The town seems content to keep it so.

Reliance

When the mines closed,
Reliance shined its shoes,
bought televisions
and got its tipple
called an Historic Place—
Today, Reliance is elegant
in its scarcity,
a tight elbow of wood
and stone and clean windows,
its walls painted yellow
to hold small light.

This brief hollow
rounds up all its dwellings
 to face the Reliance Tipple,
rusted and banging in the wind,
an odd hulk that resembles
a sky bridge between buildings,
or a church divorced from worship
by the irrelevance of coal.

Downtown, Reliance

Reliance Tipple, Reliance

Photo: Erik Molvar

Reliance Tipple, Reliance

Photo: Erik Molvar

Reliance Tipple, Reliance

SUPERIOR

41º45.783'N 108º50.050'W

Superior is located sixteen miles east of Rock Springs. To visit Superior, take Exit 122 from I-80, and follow Wyoming 371 nine miles north.

Superior, Wyoming is only nominally a ghost. There are no services other than a bar, but the town claims a population of almost 300 people. It is a beautifully situated, appealing town, and one of the most pleasant semi-ghosts in Wyoming. It is a graceful place, unpretentious and elegant in its simplicity. A good restaurant and bed-and-breakfast would do well in Superior. They might detract from the atmosphere of the town, though. It is a well-kept secret, and the residents like it that way.

In the first decade of the 20th century, coal deposits were located in the surrounding area, and Superior was founded as a coal company town. Along with Superior, a 'suburb' known as South Superior, just to the south of the original town site, was founded. South of that was a Japanese Village. The Japanese miners formed their own community. Neither South Superior nor the Japanese Village exists today. Some area locals claim that the surviving town site of Superior is South Superior.

Mining operations in Superior peaked between 1910 and 1920, when the town claimed over 1,500 residents. This presumably includes those of South Superior and the Japanese Village. Such amenities as a large miner's hall, a bowling alley, an opera house, a hospital, school, hotel, and bank were located at Superior. Other services included a saloon. This was unusual, as alcohol was generally prohibited in company towns.

Most of these structures are gone now, but the miner's hall still stands. Its ground floor has been gutted and turned into an open-air museum. It is maintained by the townspeople, as is the small, green park in the center of town.

After the coal mines played out, iron ore was mined here in limited quantities and shipped to Rock Springs by rail. All mining ceased in the Superior area in the 1970s. Superior's proximity to Rock Springs has enabled it to survive in the absence of its own industries. Many of the working inhabitants are commuters who prefer the solitude of this small, lovely community. They live in a sheltered canyon 9 miles north of I-80 on a secondary county highway that is narrow but well-maintained.

Compared to the stark landscape of Rock Springs on the open, arid plains, Superior is a bijou mountain village with a great deal of shade, peace, and quiet. There is an obvious sense of community in Superior. Hanging on the outside of one rough-hewn, hand-built cabin is a painted sign: *An Old Bear Lives Here With His Honey.*

Although I visited Superior in the early afternoon, the number of vehicles outside the one saloon identified it as a lively gathering spot for local residents. On the outskirts of Superior, on the road in, various unmarked paths lead away into scrub pine and into invisibility. These roads suggest a number of residents who find even the proximity of neighbors in tiny Superior too great. There are many interesting people who call that box canyon home. As with many semi-ghosts, Superior's charm is as pervasive as it is difficult to define.

Superior

Superior disappears,
the narrow window of road
screened with grit and snow,
the exit a thin, dirty arm
pointing to nine miles of nothing.

Halfway up the Superior road
on a generous hip of land
wild horses forage amongst glazed knobs
of sage.
Bones like fan blades, they will not gallop
away from food.
Winter is their equation:
survival = heat of energy
in their bellies, stored.
At engine sounds, they circle
the colt that leans into each of them;
their eyes cut fierce holes
into the powdered air—
A warding, laced with plea: Leave us be.
As though their lives depend
upon invisibility;
each look, each photograph,
loosens their grasp on the earth.

Superior hordes its solitude.
All its treasure dug and hauled away,

the town a looted shipwreck,
bones holding upright, an exercise of being,
this defiance of time and gravity.
Sheltered in the steep lee
of a box canyon,
Superior grows up its sides in terraces
one house deep;
American cliff dwellings, circa 1930.

Blueprint of a mining town
plain as remnant mineral tailings
from the mine:
trailers, modest homes in perpetual shade
at the bottom—
baronial stone mansions, like country inns,
claim the sunlight and view
on the topmost streets.
Turrets, edge-cut granite, stained glass—
beauty softened by wind and dryness.
Graceful ghosts, they mimic the mines:
uninhabited, no longer safe.
Their foundations stretch out
over the narrow shelf of rock:
feet on a too-short bed.
Small gardens, tangled as matted dogs,
iron gates open as dumb mouths.
Windows scoured by dust, clarity stolen
by too much wind.
These houses cannot be shored up
against erosion;

they will be dismantled
stone by stone,
or tumble, impotent,
into the lesser dwellings of the town.

In warm months, tourists dawdle
up the road
with their cameras,
snapping the gutted miners' hall,
eating sandwiches in the small, green park.

In winter, Superior is colored with quiet.
Blue coal smoke speaks softly,
doors leak scents of rosemary
and onion,
and the town breathes slow and deep
under the comfort of snow
as though, at the center of the canyon floor,
safely underground, a great furnace,
hot enough to temper glass,
feeds everything above it.

Photo: Erik Molvar

Mine Boss' House, Superior

Photo: Erik Molvar

Superior Backstreet View, Superior

Photo: Erik Molvar

Union hall, Superior

Photo: Erik Molvar

Old Stone Structure Interior, Superior

WINTON

41°44.833'N 109°10.033'W

To visit Winton, from Rock Springs take Wyoming 191 north and turn right on the Reliance road, then left on Sweetwater County Road 66, which is known locally as The Winton Road. The Winton road does not go all the way to Winton, but is a good road until the pavement ends. Beyond that the surface is hard-pack dirt and gravel. Take the Winton road to Road 18, also known as the Superior cut-off.

Road 18 is not marked, but it is the most obviously traveled of the several dirt roads leading off into canyons. The best way to know if you are heading towards Winton is to spot the railroad spur that runs parallel to the road. If there is no sign of the old railroad bed, you may be heading toward Dines or Stansbury. Neither town is posted or reported to have remains.

When you think you have taken a wrong turn and should turn around, go another mile or two and you'll most likely find yourself at Winton. Allow plenty of daylight for this trip.

Getting lost in the maze of unimproved, rocky, washed -out dirt roads around Winton would be hair-raising at night.

Located northwest of Rock Springs, Winton is a true ghost with a population of zero. There are no services nor habitable structures remaining. In its boom, the coal town of Winton supported a population of almost two thousand. The employment was exclusively dedicated to its six coal mines.

Hundreds of houses and other structures once stood in this arid, hardscrabble canyon. These boardinghouses, a school, post office, doctor's office, and pool hall are all gone. The company store, the largest building in town, is constructed of concrete. It is the last remaining structure still partially standing, though it is in ruin.

When the mines were operating, the Union Pacific ran a rail into town to collect the coal. Traces of the rail bed can be found, though the U.P. tore up and removed the tracks when it discontinued rail service to Winton.

Today, Winton is in sad shape. No signs announce its presence. The road is unmarked and in poor condition. The town site has been the teenage party hangout for many generations of Rock Springs and Reliance youth. Liberally tagged with spray paint, Winton is strewn with refuse and shotgun shells. Unlike other ghost towns, Winton is paid little respect.

Throughout the town site, it is possible to view the ruins of several buildings, one with a collapsed red tile roof. When the mines played out, most of the buildings were lifted off their stone foundations. Fitted with wheels, they were sold for a few dollars in Rock Springs, leaving many miners and their families homeless. This was, and still is, common in mining towns. This is especially true when the company owns the town and all the housing. There was no possibility of putting down permanent roots. Miners live according to the fluctuations of the industry. Winton miners were no different.

The many dirt roads that wind up and across the steep Winton town site reveal hundreds of foundations. It is difficult to imagine that there were ever more than a few isolated structures in this canyon. Proof of their existence is half-hidden by sagebrush.

Opposite the company store building, a retaining wall of solid sandstone that was built into the far canyon wall is still entirely intact. It looks like an enormous foundation, but was in fact built to shore up the steep road to the No. 1 mine.

In the gulch between the main road and the retaining wall are the remains of two vintage automobiles that lost control coming down the No. 1 mine road and landed, one on top of the other, in the ditch.

There are no signs of the bridge that once connected the main street to the mine road. It effectively cuts off access to the mines to all but the most determined hikers. Old mines are fraught with hazard, and an accident in isolated, abandoned Winton could prove fatal.

Winton's wrecked town site is fascinating to explore. The landscape has reclaimed most of the town. Scattered remnants are eerie and disconnected from their original owners. It is difficult to believe that humanity once thrived in this challenging place.

I don't believe in supernatural ghosts. Yet, when I happened upon an old, cracked baby doll, I felt a sort of unsettled presence. The porcelain face and hands were blackened and disfigured by fire. It made me glance around quickly—for what, I'm not sure.

The only surviving photographs of Winton during the

boom years assure me that Winton was once just a small, thriving Wyoming town like so many others—that it was not always so filled with ghosts.

Winton

In a cracking photo,
two pinafored girls squint into hard light
from their flowered nest
in a garden, rock-ringed
and flowing with roses
that might have been pink.

Two years later,
the coal mines dead,
all the houses were readied like boxcars
and rolled out of Winton
with wheels attached,
sold for a few dollars in Rock Springs.
Without water,
Winton relaxed into the jagged corridor
of rock and sage
it always knew itself to be,
marked human only by fences
and foundations,
dry washes filled with trucks
 flaking to cheerless confetti,
a stone wall forced into the face
of the canyon.

Winton carries the air of a place
that no one likes to speak of,

where every effort was made
to wipe away its existence.
Wind and winter have cracked this place,
leached its contents back to the rock.

Everything built here was meant
to defy transience, to write names,
indelibly, to prove heartbeat, existence,
a clinging to solid walls, to hearths,
to rituals of breakfast and washing
and the same floors, windows milky
with morning.

The scruff of wires, the jagged edges
of removal
when the Winton houses were dragged away
must have hurt the father,
so proud of his garden,
must have grieved the mother who'd buried
two infants
in rock-laced graves.
The granite ring he built to hold his roses
is full of sand and the detritus of years—
how hard to believe anything here was once
beautiful.

Not even sage grows high enough to tempt
the wind.
This crevasse fills with sharp-edged snow
six months a year;

it was not meant to host the softness
of blood and skin,
the needs of human bodies.

Still, every day before light,
the men gathered lunch pails and candles
and hoped to return,
children recited the Gettysburg Address
while chalk squeaked on slate
in the schoolhouse and the snow blew in
through chinks in the boards,
and women stoked coal stoves
through the day,
scraping frost off the windows,
baking bread and making stew,
glad for the glossy jars of last year's garden,
singing to hold down the wind,
writing letters.

And so they mourned the loss of Winton,
though it never loved them back.

Everything about its remnants speaks
of failure—
Winton crossed its arms against human
permanence,
gave its inhabitants no quarter, cast them
gladly into the wind,
erased their meager footholds,
chuffed off the detritus of roofs and wall

meant to stand for centuries
as though made of straw.
Winton scraped forgotten dolls and plates
into couloirs, covered them with sage
as though they'd never been.

Perhaps this is why Winton lies unloved
in an unmarked grave,
why it is shamed with lurid spray paint
and bejeweled with shotgun shells.
It was too hard a place
to ever gentle towards people,
to make room for all the softness
of need and want,
to yield to any kind of pressure
other than scouring heat and cold,
or its accidental namesake, the wind.

View from the Company Store Ruins, Winton

Retaining wall to Mine #1 Road, Winton

OPAL

41°46.200'N 110°19.800'W

pal is 73.5 miles from Rock Springs. To visit, take I-80 W from Rock Springs 40.7 miles to Exit 66, and US-30 W to Kemmerer/Pocatello, 31 miles. Turn Left at Chrisman St.

Opal, Wyoming, measures .43 square miles, occupying a small patch of high desert at 6,666 feet. It was founded as a stop for the Union Pacific railroad in the 1860s, and in its boom, was home to oil and railroad workers. It was also convenient to the Hams Fork River, a source of water for the railroad, which was in its own boom period. Low water levels in the Ham's Fork, then the railroad's switch from steam to oil power, closed the book on Opal's livelihood for a time.

As late as the 1920s, mineral and oil exploration were carried out near Opal, but no viable deposits were found.

The Ham's Fork Supply Company building, large and solidly built of brick, is the only permanent structure left in Opal. It is the tallest structure for many miles in either direction, and it is still an impressive sight when viewed from a distance. It was once a grocery, a saloon, a hotel, and a gas station. Now its ground floor is boarded, and the second story windows are all broken. It is a sad remnant of better, more prosperous days—the only such remnant in Opal.

There is a stone monument next to the Ham's Fork Supply Company building, dedicated to the Western pioneer. Nothing else remains to attract visitors to Opal. Several guidebooks suggest that the town's name was derived from the abundance of semi-precious stones of that name that litter the ground there. If it was once true, townspeople and tourists have since scavenged them. Wyoming natives merely smile at this legend. The correct pronunciation of Opal, they say, is 'Oh-Pal'. The claim is that an early inhabitant named it after his dog, Old Pal.

Some guidebook authors insist on the legend of opals littering the ground as common property. Wyomingites hold to the story about the old man and his dog. They are both good stories, and it is quite possible that both—or neither—is true. Buy a local old-timer a beer and ask him for the real story.

The town of Opal consists of rusting, dilapidated trailers, plywood shacks, a bar, and a lot of sagebrush, abandoned vehicles, rusted appliances, and trash. There are no trees or shade, and no services other than the unidentified bar. The Union Pacific no longer makes stops in Opal.

The town's location, at the junction of Highway 30 and State Highway 240, is far enough away from any other settlement that it could easily support a few services. Opal is now becoming a natural gas hub. If someone with vision and resources, and a love for the high plains, took up the challenge, perhaps Opal could be reborn into a small gem of a town.

It would be wonderful to see the solid old Hamm's Fork

Supply Company building, with its good brick walls, become the center of commerce in this small town again. It would make a wonderful hotel, with a restaurant on the ground floor. Since the natural gas business has taken off in Opal, incomes and housing prices have tripled. Perhaps a renaissance is just around the corner; this would be even better than a strewing of precious stones across the desert.

Opal

Gray skin of dank snow,
accretion of fence-blown garbage
like flies at the corners of a mouth.
Cluster of trailers, paint-peeled,
floors lined with cardboard,
an ugly crust on the face of any season.

The rusted town sign
rescinds its invitation
to passersby.
Opal's lore, a strewing
of precious stones,
sings sweetly to visitors
it cannot keep.

The old store
from the boom days
is losing its edges, its broken windows
staring hopefully at nothing.
Only pervasive lack of paint
has saved it from graffiti,
but good, strong walls wait
to hold a new life
inside them.

An amazing absence of trees:
no effort made here

to gentle the Opal wind
that shoves a hand
in every pocket.

If there were a loose edge, a thread
at the corner of Opal,
it could be pulled loose, the whole
settlement with its dead cars and twisted
trailers
unraveled,
leaving the prairie
to shake itself clean
come spring.

Photo: Erik Molvar

Hamm's Fork Store, Opal

Photo: Erik Molvar

Outbuilding, Opal

PIEDMONT

41º12.934'N 110º37.661'W

Piedmont is located in the extreme southwest corner of Wyoming, near the Utah state line. To visit Piedmont, take exit #24 from I-80, and go approximately 7 miles south on this gravel road that was once the railroad bed. It is elevated ten feet above the prairie. A lack of caution could cause a rollover, so drive cautiously on the Piedmont road.

The town site is on private land, but the main road runs through the middle of it. Respectful and tidy visitors are not discouraged from taking a closer look at the structures and cemeteries. The charcoal kilns are open to visitors. You may tour the kiln site, and informative historical markers describe their building and purpose.

The dirt track leading up to the Byrne-Hinesdale Cemetery is rutted and unimproved. Four-wheel drive may be required at any time of year to drive to it, but it is near enough to the town site to hike in.

Piedmont, Wyoming is a true ghost, tucked into a slim valley between rolling hills. Its only inhabitants are a herd of glossy black cattle and those who have long lain in the two cemeteries. Founded in 1868 by Moses Byrne and his wife, Catherine Byrne, Piedmont was first the site of an Overland stage station. Later, it was a whistle stop of the Union Pacific Railroad.

Moses Byrne, an Irish sea captain, was drawn to the American West after his conversion to the Mormon faith. He met Catherine, who had also been converted by Mormon missionaries, on the wagon train heading west. They married shortly after arriving in Salt Lake City, Utah. Two months later, he married another woman, Anne, whom he also met on the wagon train.

With Catherine, Moses Byrne traveled to Wyoming, leaving Anne behind in Salt Lake City.

Moses Byrne built five charcoal smelters along the narrow river in Piedmont. It was named for the region of Italy where Catherine and her sister were born. Originally called Byrne, the town's name had to be changed due to confusion with a nearby town called Bryan.

The remaining structures in Piedmont are relatively well-preserved, though none are habitable. A few houses and a barn are yet standing, and were at one time all identified with historical markers, though many of these seem to have been taken by souvenir seekers. The Willie Byrne House is still marked. It is the burial site of one of the Byrne women who died during winter and was interred under a corner of the house.

The size and apparent quality of the structures—some of them two-story houses—suggests that the Byrne family was quite successful. Moses and Catherine Byrne worked tirelessly to increase their land holdings. Moses' charcoal smelters supplied crucial fuel for the engines. That was, until the Union Pacific moved the rail line.

In later years, Moses and Catherine Byrne accumulated significant land holdings in and around Piedmont. The land around it is still ranched by Byrne descendants.

The cemeteries in Piedmont tell a brutal story in great, sorrowful detail, just as other ghost cemeteries do. The vast majority of those who rest there are women and children lost in childbirth and to childhood illnesses long since conquered by modern medicine.

Piedmont, even today, is extremely isolated from major roads and towns. When it was founded, the nearest emergency services were in Utah. Illness and emergencies in Piedmont, as in so many frontier settlements, too often ended in unnecessary deaths.

Catherine Byrne, though she endured the loss of many of her children, thrived into her eighth decade. Moses Byrne also lived a long and industrious life. His other wife, Anne, remained in Salt Lake City, near her parents. She bore Moses at least eight children beyond the thirteen he fathered with Catherine. Moses visited Anne on occasional supply trips, but she never lived in Piedmont.

Today, Piedmont is quiet and lovely, particularly in the summer. It is a narrow valley, terraced upward in verdant pastures and traced with a slim, deep river. It is an excellent day trip for anyone who enjoys the peace and historical traces of those who settled the high plains.

Piedmont

Beehive kilns stand silent,
gray as storm-sky, gray
as washer-women,
arches blackened, cracking.
Their insides clabbered
with mud-swallows,
only memory could make them beautiful.
Moses Byrne touched every part of his kilns,
assembled the cold stones
like a history of Ireland.

Oh, the trees.
The wagons came drunk with trees
like bakers with arms full of bread
to kilns reeking hollow
with a new definition of heat.
Night and day, the molasses stink
of charred pine.
In houses across the road,
Byrne women slept little,
dreaming of house fires.
When the rains came,
river and faces
ran dark.
The kilns shivered,
silver with steam.

That lost town, Piedmont,
now a crease between hills,
loam stoked with charcoal,
grasses growing long.
Behind the kilns,
fields terrace upward
to wrap the cemetery
like a gift.

Catherine Byrne bore thirteen children,
and too many in winter.
She had the strength to call
the last of four stillborn babies
Joy.
She lay each infant
inside its blue-white shroud,
wrapped them like flowers
closing at dusk.
Even the graves are stained
with charcoal,
though Catherine planted
black-veined moss
to draw away the dust.

Piedmont breathes free now,
the air around the kilns blown clean
as cold water,
the fields thick and smooth as pelts,
fat black cows chewing
in cathedral silence.

Every distance stretches
equally
from Catherine's stone,
the dustless white of it glowing
like bright-work
In this sheltered seam
between mountains.

The kilns stand still,
out of time in their strangeness,
monuments to a captain
who burned enough trees
to quench a sea
left behind
on the strength
of a mortal man's stories
of God.

Photo: Erik Molvar

Surviving buildings, Piedmont

Photo: Erik Molvar

Charcoal kilns, Piedmont

Photo: Erik Molvar

Old home, Piedmont

Photo: Erik Molvar

Ranch view, Piedmont

Afterword

This book would not have been possible without funding from the Wyoming Arts Council. Other crucial resources were provided by numerous county and town museums that are dedicated to preserving the legacy of Wyoming's earliest towns and settlements, and they are excellent places to visit if you are in the area. The museum in Hanna, Wyoming, serves as an archive for many towns that have all but disappeared.

The Medicine Bow museum offers a smaller but well-managed archive, and the Rock Springs Historical Museum can provide you with information on outlying ghost towns as well. Beyond these formal repositories of history, though, you will likely find someone in every diner, remote gas station, library or bar across the state, eager to share local history and disclose some hard-to-come-by information about the nearby ghost towns.

If *Voices at Twilight* helps you find your way to some of these isolated ghosts, remember to travel safely, watch out for inclement weather, and take away only what you can store in your camera.

Safe travels—
Lori Howe

Acknowledgments

This book would not have come to fruition without the advice, guidance, mentorship, funding, friendship, knowledge, and community support of a great many friends and colleagues. My thanks to the University of Wyoming M.F.A. in Creative Writing program and English Department. Both played enormous roles in my becoming a poet and writer, and I thank them for support, encouragement, and research funding as I traveled Wyoming's back roads, researching and writing the poems and essays in this collection.

Particular thanks to UW M.F.A. faculty David Romtvedt, Brad Watson, Alyson Hagy, and Harvey Hix, and past and present English faculty Peter Parolin, Caroline McCracken-Flesher, Susan Aronstein, Julianne Couch, the late Robert Tory, and Paisley Rekdal. Continuing thanks, also, to the University of Wyoming College of Education and Literacy Studies Program, for their continued support as I pursue both my doctorate and the best ways to bring the joys of writing to the good people of Wyoming. Many thanks, also, to the Wyoming Arts Council for support in the form of an Individual Artist Development grant, and to the Wyoming Humanities Council for selecting me as a 2016 ThinkWY Roads Scholar. I appreciate you all, so very much, for supporting poets and writers in Wyoming.

Special thanks to Bob Beck at Wyoming Public Radio for inviting me to read poems from *Cloudshade* and *Voices at Twilight* on Open Spaces, and for generously promoting arts and writing events in Wyoming, including my own.

Thanks also to all the administrators, volunteers, and archivists in the museums great and small around the state of Wyoming, who so graciously helped me find the old documents and records that made an accurate depiction of these towns possible, and for fact-checking my historical essays. My heartfelt appreciation, also, to the good folks across Wyoming who live in or near the towns and town sites in this book, who gave me several ears-full of directions, advice, little-known facts, and tours of places I would never have seen, and for pulling me out of the ditch, correcting my pronunciation, and otherwise setting me straight.

Additional thanks to local Laramie businesses Night Heron Books, Chalk 'N Cheese, Coal Creek Coffee, and Hastings, for hosting events promoting *Voices at Twilight* and *Cloudshade: Poems of the High Plains.* You make Laramie a great place for the arts.

Special thanks to friends and writing group members Jason Deiss, Heather Gallardo, Sunnie Gaylord, and Oscar Lilley, for nearly a decade of friendship and membership in our wonderful community of practice. *To the moon and back, all of you.*

A whole world of gratitude to my amazing, professional publisher Sastrugi Press. Working with you on these books is one of the great joys of my life. Thank you.

Above all, my deepest thanks to Erik, my wonderful partner and champion, who steadfastly believed that I could and would publish two books in one year—and during my doctoral program, no less. His stunning photographs grace these pages and help to illuminate the spirit of the landscape, interwoven with the lives and legacies of those who've come before us.

Enjoy other Sastrugi Press titles

Cloudshade by Lori Howe

In every season, life on America's high plains is at once harsh and beautiful, liberating and isolated, welcoming and unforgiving. The poems of Cloudshade take us through those seasons, illuminating the intersections between the landscapes surrounding us and those inside us. Extraordinarily relatable, the poems of Cloudshade swing wide a door to life in the West, both for lovers of poetry and for those who don't normally read poems. Available in print and audiobook formats.

These Canyons Are Full of Ghosts by Emmett Harder

Driven to find his fortune in the most desolate and forbidding landscapes on earth, one prospector learns there is more to finding gold than just using a shovel and pickaxe. While exploring the massive national park, Emmett Harder crosses paths with Death Valley's most notorious resident: Charles Manson.

Journeys to the Edge by Randall Peeters, PhD.

Ever wonder what it's like to climb Mount Everest? The idea isn't as far-fetched as it may seem, even though very few people in the world have climbed Mount Everest. It requires dreaming big and creating a personal vision to climb the mountains in your life. Randall Peeters shares his guidelines to create a personal vision.

The Blind Man's Story by J.W. Linsdau

Imagine one's surprise to be hiking in the great Northwest and coming across someone who is blind and spends his summers living high on a mountain. That's what happened to journalist

Beau Larson. He returns to work to cover a dispute between local timber workers and environmentalists. Beau finishes his report, but soon discovers there is more to the story than he thought.

Antarctic Tears by Aaron Linsdau

What would make someone give up a high-paying career to ski across Antarctica alone? This inspirational true story will make readers both cheer and cry. Fighting skin-freezing temperatures, infections, and emotional breakdown, Aaron Linsdau exposes harsh realities of the world's largest wilderness. Discover what drives someone to the brink of destruction while pursing a dream. Available in print and audiobook formats.

Roaming the Wild by Grover Ratliff

Jackson Hole is home to some of the most iconic landscapes in North America. In this land of harsh winters and short summers, wildlife survive and thrive. People from all around the world travel here to savor both the rare vistas of the high Rockies and have the chance to observe bear, moose and elk. It is an environment like no other, covered in snow most of the year yet blanketed by wildflowers for a few precious months. This place is both powerful and delicate.

Visit Sastrugi Press on the web at www.sastrugipress.com to purchase the above titles directly from the publisher. They are also available from your local bookstore or online retailers in print or ebook form.

Thank you for choosing Sastrugi Press.

CPSIA information can be obtained
at www.ICGtesting.com
Printed in the USA
LVOW06s0738100517

533817LV00009B/25/P